D0460691

EXPLORING SPACE

Mars

by Derek Zobel

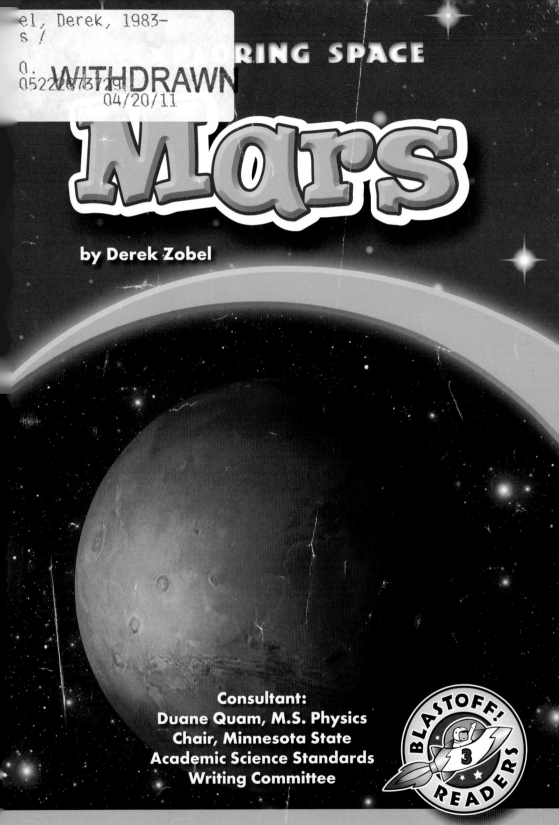

Consultant:
Duane Quam, M.S. Physics
Chair, Minnesota State
Academic Science Standards
Writing Committee

BLASTOFF!
3
READERS

BELLWETHER MEDIA · MINNEAPOLIS, MN

Note to Librarians, Teachers, and Parents:

Blastoff! Readers are carefully developed by literacy experts and combine standards-based content with developmentally appropriate text.

Level 1 provides the most support through repetition of high-frequency words, light text, predictable sentence patterns, and strong visual support.

Level 2 offers early readers a bit more challenge through varied simple sentences, increased text load, and less repetition of high-frequency words.

Level 3 advances early-fluent readers toward fluency through increased text and concept load, less reliance on visuals, longer sentences, and more literary language.

Level 4 builds reading stamina by providing more text per page, increased use of punctuation, greater variation in sentence patterns, and increasingly challenging vocabulary.

Level 5 encourages children to move from "learning to read" to "reading to learn" by providing even more text, varied writing styles, and less familiar topics.

Whichever book is right for your reader, Blastoff! Readers are the perfect books to build confidence and encourage a love of reading that will last a lifetime!

This edition first published in 2010 by Bellwether Media, Inc.

No part of this publication may be reproduced in whole or in part without written permission of the publisher. For information regarding permission, write to Bellwether Media, Inc., Attention: Permissions Department, 5357 Penn Avenue South, Minneapolis, MN 55419.

Library of Congress Cataloging-in-Publication Data

Zobel, Derek, 1983-
Mars / by Derek Zobel.
   p. cm. – (Blastoff! readers. Exploring space)
Includes bibliographical references and index.
Summary: "Introductory text and full-color images explore the physical characteristics and discovery of the planet Mars. Intended for students in kindergarten through third grade"–Provided by publisher.
ISBN 978-1-60014-405-9 (hardcover : alk. paper)
1. Mars (Planet)–Juvenile literature. I. Title.
QB641.Z63 2010
523.43–dc22   2009042747

Contents

Mars is a **planet** in the **solar system**. It is named after the **Roman god** of war.

It is sometimes called the "Red Planet" because of its red surface.

All of the planets **orbit** the sun. Mars is the fourth planet from the sun.

Mars

Mars has an oval-shaped orbit. It lies between 128 million and 155 million miles (207 and 249 kilometers) from the sun.

axis

The time it takes a planet to orbit the sun once is called a year. Mars completes an orbit of the sun in 687 Earth days.

Mars spins on its **axis** as it orbits the sun. One spin is called a day. A day on Mars is about 25 Earth hours.

Canyons, mountains, **craters**, and rocky plains make up the surface of Mars. The surface is covered with a reddish dust.

Olympus Mons

Mars has the largest mountain in the solar system. It is called Olympus Mons. It is 17 miles (27 kilometers) tall!

Mars has a stretch of canyons
called the Valles Marineris.
It is over 2,500 miles (4,000
kilometers) long.

The canyons are 370 miles (600 kilometers) across at the widest point. Some canyons are 5 to 6 miles (8 to 10 kilometers) deep!

Mars also has ice caps.
They lie at the top and
bottom of the planet.

ice caps

Asaph Hall

Astronomer Asaph Hall discovered two **moons** around Mars in 1877. He named them Phobos and Deimos.

Phobos and Deimos are shaped like potatoes. Some scientists think they were **asteroids** captured by Mars' **gravity**.

Phobos

Deimos

rover

Scientists have sent **space probes** and **rovers** to Mars. These tools help scientists learn more about planets.

space probe

Space probes orbit Mars to map the surface and take photographs.

Rovers roll across the surface of Mars. Scientists use them to take pictures and study the soil and **atmosphere**.

Some people think **astronauts** should be sent to Mars. The journey would take about one year.

The astronauts would be the first people to ever walk on another planet!

Glossary

asteroids—space rocks that orbit the sun

astronauts—people who have been trained to fly aboard a space shuttle and work in space

astronomer—a scientist who studies space and objects in space

atmosphere—the gases around an object in space

axis—an imaginary line that runs through the center of a planet; a planet spins on its axis.

craters—holes made when meteorites or other space objects crash into moons, planets, or other objects

gravity—the force that pulls objects toward each other; gravity keeps objects from moving away in space.

moons—space objects that orbit a planet or other space object

orbit—to travel around the sun or other object in space

planet—a large, round space object that revolves around the sun and is alone in its orbit

Roman god—a god worshipped by the people of ancient Rome; Mars was the Roman god of war.

rovers—probes that land on the surface of a space object and explore to gather information

solar system—the sun and all the objects that orbit it; the solar system has planets, moons, comets, and asteroids.

space probes—spacecraft that explore planets and other space objects and send information back to Earth; space probes do not carry people.

To Learn More

AT THE LIBRARY

Jefferies, David. *Mars: Distant Red Planet*. New York, N.Y.: Crabtree Publishing, 2008.

O'Brien, Patrick. *You Are the First Kid on Mars*. New York, N.Y.: G.P. Putnam's Sons, 2009.

Siy, Alexandra. *Cars on Mars: Roving the Red Planet*. Watertown, Mass.: Charlesbridge Publishing, 2009.

ON THE WEB

Learning more about Mars is as easy as 1, 2, 3.

1. Go to www.factsurfer.com.

2. Enter "Mars" into the search box.

3. Click the "Surf" button and you will see a list of related Web sites.

With factsurfer.com, finding more information is just a click away.

BLASTOFF! JIMMY CHALLENGE

Blastoff! Jimmy is hidden somewhere in this book. Can you find him? If you need help, you can find a hint at the bottom of page 24.

Index

The images in this book are reproduced through the courtesy of: Juan Martinez, front cover, pp. 4-5, 10-11; Timur Kulgarin, p. 4 (small); NASA, pp. 6-7, 17, 18, 19, 20 (small); Detlev van Ravenswaay / Science Photo Library, pp. 11 (small), 14-15; Fotosearch, pp. 12-13; Science Source / Science Photo Library, p. 15 (small); De Agostini / Getty Images, pp. 16-17; Antonio M. Rosario, pp. 20-21.

Blastoff! Jimmy Challenge (from page 23).
Hint: Go to page 8 and shoot for the stars.